Bible Dayze!

BY
darren

Kevin
Mayhew

First published in 1996 by
KEVIN MAYHEW LTD
Rattlesden
Bury St Edmunds
Suffolk IP30 0SZ

0 1 2 3 4 5 6 7 8 9

ISBN 0 86209 923 4
Catalogue No 1500083

Cover illustration by Darren
Edited by David Gatward
Typesetting by Louise Hill
Printed and bound in Great Britain by
Caligraving Limited Thetford Norfolk

to God
for the original material

Through scarlet blind summers
red wine and lost lovers

for Brent – my friend

Foreword by

SIMON MAYO

I have, to be honest, always found biblical illustrations
rather rubbish. Washed-up hippies and drug-addled
long-hair types in sheets for disciples, fey, pale Englishmen or
70s folk singer-songwriters for Jesus, all cheek-by-jowl
with an assortment of stick men and women
for Noah, Jonah, Balaam's ass, etc.

Now, if a Bible were to have illustrations like Darren's
here, it could get quite popular . . .

MATTHEW 14 vv. 15-21

Jesus wanted to be alone but a crowd of over five thousand people soon gathered. When evening came the disciples went to Jesus and reported that the people were growing hungry, yet the only food available was the five loaves and two fishes brought by a young boy. Jesus took the loaves and the fish, looked up to heaven and gave thanks, then he passed them to his disciples to give to the people. They all ate plenty and were satisfied.

FEEDING THE FIVE THOUSAND

EXODUS 2 vv. 1-10

To save baby Moses from certain
death, his mother placed him in
a papyrus basket and hid him in
the reeds of the Nile. Now when
Pharaoh's daughter went to the
Nile to bathe she saw the
basket and sent her servants to
retrieve it. She took pity on the
baby and eventually adopted
Moses as her own son.

WORD SOON GOT OUT OF A WAY IN WHICH BABIES COULD BE ACCEPTED INTO PHARAOH'S PALACE

1 SAMUEL 17 v. 4

A champion named Goliath, who was a giant from Gath, came out of the Philistine camp.

GOLIATH AND FAMILY AT HOME

JOHN 5 vv. 2-4

In Jerusalem there is a pool
called Bethesda where a great
number of sick and disabled
people used to come to wait for
the moving of the waters. From
time to time an angel of the Lord
came down and stirred up the
waters. Then the first of the
people into the pool would be
healed.

AT THE POOL OF BETHESDA

GENESIS 3 vv. 1-6

God gave to the man and the woman the Garden of Eden to care for and he said to them, 'You are free to eat from any tree in the garden, but you must not eat from the Tree of the Knowledge of Good and Evil.'

The serpent, who was more crafty than any of the other animals God had made, came to the woman to tempt her to eat the fruit from the forbidden tree.

PROBLEMS IN EDEN

GENESIS 6 v. 19

God spoke to Noah, saying, 'You
are to bring into the ark two of all
living creatures, male and female,
to keep them alive with you.'

ROUNDING UP THE ANIMALS — PART ONE
NOAH AND THE BUTTERFLIES

GENESIS 41 v. 14

So Pharaoh sent for Joseph, and he was quickly brought from the dungeon. When he had shaved and changed his clothes, he came before Pharaoh.

JOSEPH MAKES A BIT OF A FAUX PAS

MATTHEW 2 v. 11

Wise men came to the stable where Jesus was born, and they bowed down and worshipped him. Then they opened their treasures and presented him with gifts of gold, frankincense, and myrrh.

MERCENARY LIVESTOCK

ACTS 10 vv. 9-16

At noon the next day, Peter
went up onto the roof to pray.
There he saw a vision – some-
thing like a large sheet being let
down to earth from heaven and
it held all kinds of four-footed
animals, as well as reptiles and
birds. Then a voice told him,
'Get up, Peter, kill and eat.'

IN HIS SECOND VISION PETER WAS PRESENTED
WITH A FINE SELECTION OF DESSERTS, FOLLOWED
BY A THIRD IN WHICH HE SAW TEA, COFFEE AND
VARIOUS ASSORTED MINTS

EXODUS 4 vv. 1-3

Moses said to God, 'What if they do not believe me?'
So the Lord asked him, 'What is that in your hand?'
'A rod,' Moses replied.
'Cast it down on the ground,' said the Lord. So Moses cast the rod to the ground and it became a snake.

MARK 5 vv. 11-13

When Jesus entered Gerasenes
he was met by a man filled with
evil spirits. Jesus ordered the
spirits to leave the man, sending
them into a herd of pigs that was
feeding on a nearby hillside.

GENESIS 27 vv. 12-24

As Isaac was old and his eyes
were weak, Jacob planned to
trick his father into giving him
his brother Esau's birthright
and blessing. Jacob said to his
mother, Rebekah, 'My brother
is a hairy man but I am a man
with smooth skin; what if my
father touches me? He will
realise I am not Esau after all!'
So Rebekah put goat skins on
Jacob to disguise his smooth
skin and then sent him to his
father.

JACOB DOES NOT GET ISAAC'S BLESSING

1 SAMUEL 19 v. 9

As David was playing the harp, an evil spirit came upon Saul causing him to try and pin David to the wall with his spear.

THE REAL REASON SAUL TRIED TO KILL DAVID

ISAIAH 11 v. 6

A day will come when the wild
animals will live with the tame
and the fierce creatures will lay
down with the gentle.

MARK 2 vv. 4-5

Since they could not get the paralysed man to Jesus because of the crowd, his friends made a hole in the roof above Jesus and lowered him on his mat into the room. Jesus saw their faith and he healed the man.

MOMENTS LATER THE ROOF FELL IN AND BILL BROKE HIS OTHER LEG

JUDGES 16 v. 17

When Israel was again in
desperate trouble, God gave to a
man and his wife a son called
Samson. Samson was to be set
aside for God and if his hair
remained untouched by a razor
or blade he was to possess
incredible strength.

SAMSON AT HOME

GENESIS 6 v. 19

God spoke to Noah, saying, 'You are to bring into the ark two of all living creatures, male and female, to keep them alive with you.'

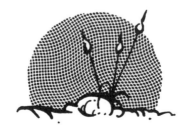

ROUNDING UP THE ANIMALS - PART TWO
NOAH AND THE BEES

JOHN 2 vv. 1-10

On the third day Jesus and his
disciples went to a wedding in
Galilee. After a time the wine
ran out and Mary came to Jesus
for help. Jesus said to the
servants, 'Fill these stone jars to
the brim with water.' They did
as Jesus said, but on drawing the
water from the jars they found it
had turned into wine.

BEARING THE CHILDREN IN MIND, JESUS DIDN'T TURN ALL OF THE WATER INTO WINE

LUKE 15 vv. 11-32

Jesus then told the parable of
the prodigal son who left his
father's house with his inheri-
tance. Soon, however, he had
wasted all his money and was
starving. The son reasoned that
he could return to his father's
house and beg his father to take
him back as one of the servants.
As he neared the house, however,
his father saw him coming and
instead of being angry he ran to
meet his son and embraced him.
'Quick,' he called to the servants, 'bring the best robe and
put it on him. Put a ring on his
finger and sandals on his feet.
Bring the fattened calf and kill
it. Let's have a feast and cele-
brate, for this son of mine was
dead and is alive again; he was
lost and is found.'

GENESIS 19 vv. 24-25

Then the Lord rained down
burning sulphur on Sodom and
Gomorrah. Thus he overthrew
those cities and the entire plain,
including all those living in the
cities and also the vegetation on
the land.

GENESIS 37 v. 3

Jacob loved Joseph more than all
his other children and he made
him a coat of many colours.

TRY AS HE MIGHT JACOB JUST COULDN'T GET IT RIGHT

JOHN 9 vv. 6-7

Then a man blind from birth
came to Jesus so that he might
be healed. Jesus spat on the
ground making clay from the
saliva and soil and put it in the
man's eyes. 'Go,' he told him,
'wash in the pool of Siloam.'

1 SAMUEL 17 v. 49

David went out to fight the Philistine giant with only a sling and five smooth stones. As Goliath moved towards him, David took a stone, placed it in his sling and flung it, striking the giant on the forehead.

DAVID INADVERTENTLY DISCOVERS THE TRUTH ABOUT 'GOLIATH'

GENESIS 8 v. 8

Noah sent out a dove from the ark to see if the waters had receded from the surface of the ground.

IT SEEMED LIKELY THAT NOAH'S DOVE HAD
INDEED DISCOVERED SOME DRY GROUND

DANIEL 6 vv. 16-22

So the king, against his will, gave the order that Daniel was to be thrown into the lions' den. The king prayed for Daniel all night and in the morning he ran to the den calling, 'Daniel, has your God been able to rescue you from the lions?' Daniel answered, 'Oh king, my God sent his angel to protect me from the lions and they have not harmed me.'

DANIEL IS SAVED FROM THE LIONS

ACTS 12 vv. 6-11

The night before Herod was to bring him to trial, Peter was asleep in his cell, chained and guarded. Suddenly an angel of the Lord appeared and struck Peter on the side. 'Quick, get up!' he said, and the chains fell off Peter's wrists. 'Put your cloak and sandals on and follow me.' Peter did as the angel instructed and together they passed through the prison and out into the city and not one of the guards was able to see them. When they had walked the length of the street, the angel left Peter.

UNFORTUNATELY THE ANGEL THOUGHT THE LORD HAD SAID "THIRD ON THE LEFT" AND, WHILST PETER SLEPT, PHIL 'THE FIST' MAGRAW MADE AN UNEXPECTED ESCAPE FROM HEROD'S JAIL

GENESIS 19 vv. 17, 24-26

With the coming of dawn the
angels urged Lot and his wife,
saying, 'Hurry, or you will be
swept away when the city is
punished. Flee for your lives
and do not look back.' Then
the Lord rained down burning sulphur on Sodom and
Gomorrah, but Lot's wife looked
back and she became a pillar of
salt.

WHAT BECAME OF LOT'S WIFE

MATTHEW 2 vv. 1-2

Following the birth of Jesus in Bethlehem in Judea, Magi from the East came to Jerusalem to worship him.

NUMBERS 22 v. 28

So that Balaam's disobedience might be revealed, the Lord opened his donkey's mouth and caused it to speak to him.

LUKE 4 vv. 1-2

Jesus returned from the Jordan
and was led by the spirit into
the desert where for forty days
he was tempted by the devil.

UNDOCUMENTED TEMPTATIONS OF JESUS

GENESIS 6 v. 19

God spoke to Noah, saying, 'You
are to bring into the ark two of all
living creatures, male and female,
to keep them alive with you.'

ROUNDING UP THE ANIMALS - PART THREE
NOAH AND THE PENGUINS

MATTHEW 3 v. 4

John's clothes were made of
camels' hair and he had a
leather belt around his waist.
His food was locusts and wild
honey.

THE DISCIPLES HATED DINNER ROUND AT
JOHN THE BAPTIST'S

EXODUS 15 vv. 23-26

When they came to Marah the
people could not drink the
water because it was bitter. The
people grumbled to Moses and
he cried out to the Lord. Then
the Lord showed Moses a piece
of wood which he threw into the
waters and they became sweet
to drink.

MOSES IS FACED WITH ANOTHER OPPORTUNITY TO USE HIS WOOD FOR THE BENEFIT OF OTHERS

GENESIS 37 v. 3

Jacob loved Joseph more than all
his other children and he made
him a coat of many colours.

IT WASN'T LONG BEFORE JOSEPH'S COAT CAUGHT ON

JOHN 11 vv. 38-43

Jesus was saddened by the death of Lazarus and he went to the tomb, commanding that the stone should be removed from the entrance. 'But Lord,' said Martha, 'by this time there is a bad odour for he has been there four days.'

Jesus replied, 'Did I not tell you that if you believed you would see the glory of God?' Then Jesus prayed and called out in a loud voice, 'Lazarus, come out . . .'

THE EMBARRASSMENT OF RESURRECTION

EXODUS 8 v. 21

God instructed Moses to speak
to Pharaoh, saying, 'This is what
the Lord says: "If you do not let
my people go, I will send
swarms of flies on you and your
officials, on your people and
into your homes. The houses of
the Egyptians will be full of
flies and cover even the ground
where they stand."'

ALTHOUGH A GREAT IRRITATION TO MOST
THE PLAGUE OF FLIES WAS A POSITIVE
BOON TO SOME

JUDGES 15 vv. 4-5

Samson went out and caught
three hundred foxes and tied
them tail to tail in pairs. He
then fastened a torch to each
pair of tails, lit the torches and
let the foxes loose in the
standing corn of the Philistines.

SAMSON'S UNUSUAL MEANS OF FIRELIGHTING WAS SURE TO IMPRESS HIS DATES

LUKE 9 vv. 14-16

Jesus took the five loaves and
the two fishes and lifted them
up to heaven, giving thanks.
When the disciples distributed
the food among the crowd, all
five thousand people were fed
and satisfied.

JOHN 2 vv. 7-9

Jesus said to the servants, 'Fill
these stone jars to the brim with
water.' When they did as he
commanded the water became
wine.

JONAH 1 v. 17

The Lord provided a great fish
to swallow Jonah and he was
inside the fish for three days
and three nights.

JONAH'S LAST DAYS

1 KINGS 17 vv. 1-6

Elijah went to the wilderness east of the Jordan and there the Lord sent the ravens to bring him bread and meat in the mornings and evenings.

HAVING LEFT THE WILDERNESS ELIJAH FELT IT
WAS ONLY RIGHT THAT HE RETURNED THE FAVOUR

GENESIS 11 v. 4

The people of the place that
became Babel said to each
other, 'Come, let us build our-
selves a city with a tower that
reaches to the heavens.'

WORKING ON THE TOWER OF BABEL

LUKE 2 v. 7

Mary gave birth to her firstborn,
a son, and she placed him in a
manger for there was no room in
the inn.

THE THREE KINGS DISCOVER THEY'RE AT
THE WRONG STABLE

1 SAMUEL 17 vv. 34-35

David said to Saul, 'Your servant has been keeping his father's sheep. When a lion or bear came and carried off a sheep from the flock, I went after it, struck it and rescued the sheep from its mouth. When it turned on me, I seized it by its hair, struck it and killed it.'

THE BEARS COULD NO LONGER RELY ON
THEIR 'WALTZ-IN-AND-GRAB-A-SHEEP' PLAN

JUDGES 6 vv. 36-40

To seek confirmation of God's promises, Gideon took a fleece and placed it on the ground. 'If there is dew only on the fleece and none on the ground,' Gideon said, 'I will know that you have spoken, Lord.'

In the morning this was exactly how Gideon found the fleece. 'Allow me to make another request,' Gideon asked, wanting to be completely sure. 'If there is dew on the ground tomorrow morning, but none on the fleece, then I will be sure.' And again it was exactly so the next morning.

GIDEON WASN'T ONE TO TAKE CHANCES

GENESIS 6 v. 19

God spoke to Noah, saying, 'You
are to bring into the ark two of all
living creatures, male and female,
to keep them alive with you.'

ROUNDING UP THE ANIMALS- PART FOUR
NOAH AND THE CHAMELEONS

thanks to all my friends and family for
   their encouragement over the years ———
   special thanks to mum & dad, amber & sam,
roger (tanti—) and clair, and to jeremy;
for being on my wave length, matt — for
   the friendship (and c.d.'s) and finally
      to ruth — " for the all and the
   more that you are "